Greater Than a Tourist Book Series
Reviews from Readers

I think the series is wonderful and beneficial for tourists to get information before visiting the city.

-Seckin Zumbul, Izmir Turkey

I am a world traveler who has read many trip guides but this one really made a difference for me. I would call it a heartfelt creation of a local guide expert instead of just a guide.

-Susy, Isla Holbox, Mexico

New to the area like me, this is a must have!

 -Joe, Bloomington, USA

This is a good series that gets down to it when looking for things to do at your destination without having to read a novel for just a few ideas.

-Rachel, Monterey, USA

Good information to have to plan my trip to this destination.

-Pennie Farrell, Mexico

Great ideas for a port day.

-Mary Martin USA

Aptly titled, you won't just be a tourist after reading this book. You'll be greater than a tourist!

-Alan Warner, Grand Rapids, USA

Even though I only have three days to spend in San Miguel in an upcoming visit, I will use the author's suggestions to guide some of my time there. An easy read - with chapters named to guide me in directions I want to go.

 -Robert Catapano, USA

Great insights from a local perspective! Useful information and a very good value!

 -Sarah, USA

This series provides an in-depth experience through the eyes of a local. Reading these series will help you to travel the city in with confidence and it'll make your journey a unique one.

-Andrew Teoh, Ipoh, Malaysia

GREATER THAN A TOURIST- KANSAS CITY MISSOURI USA

50 Travel Tips from a Local

Isaiah Tribelhorn

Cover designed by: Ivana Stamenkovic
Cover Image: https://pixabay.com/photos/kansas-city-city-skyline-missouri-4564805/

Image 1:
https://commons.wikimedia.org/wiki/File:Westport_Pioneers_Statue.jpg
User:Charvex [Public domain]
Image 2: https://commons.wikimedia.org/wiki/File:Penn_Valley_Park.jpg Brit
By Birth [CC BY-SA (https://creativecommons.org/licenses/by-sa/4.0)]
Image 3:
https://en.wikipedia.org/wiki/File:Country_Club_Plaza_2_Kansas_City_MO.jpg
User:Charvex [Public domain]
Image 4:
https://en.wikipedia.org/wiki/File:Crown_Center_1_Kansas_City_MO.jpg
User:Charvex [Public domain]

CZYK Publishing Since 2011.
Greater Than a Tourist

Lock Haven, PA
All rights reserved.

ISBN: 9798607962517

>TOURIST

50 TRAVEL TIPS FROM A LOCAL

BOOK DESCRIPTION

With travel tips and culture in our guidebooks written by a local, it is never too late to visit Kansas City. Greater Than a Tourist- Kansas City, Missouri, United States of America, by Author Isaiah Tribelhorn offers the inside scoop on Missouri's largest cityscape.

Most travel books tell you how to travel like a tourist. Although there is nothing wrong with that, as part of the 'Greater Than a Tourist' series, this book will give you candid travel tips from someone who has lived at your next travel destination. This guide book will not tell you exact addresses or store hours but instead gives you knowledge that you may not find in other smaller print travel books. Experience cultural, culinary delights, and attractions like with guidance from a Local. Slow down and get to know the people with this invaluable guide. By the time you finish this book, you will be eager and prepared to discover new activities at your next travel destination.

Inside this travel guide book you will find:

Visitor information from a Local
Tour ideas and inspiration
Save time with valuable guidebook information

Greater Than a Tourist- A Travel Guidebook with 50 Travel Tips from a Local. Slow down, stay in one place, and get to know the people and culture. By the time you finish this book, you will be eager and prepared to travel to your next destination.

OUR STORY

Traveling is a passion of the Greater than a Tourist book series creator. Lisa studied abroad in college, and for their honeymoon Lisa and her husband toured Europe. During her travels to Malta, an older man tried to give her some advice based on his own experience living on the island since he was a young boy. She was not sure if she should talk to the stranger but was interested in his advice. When traveling to some places she was wary to talk to locals because she was afraid that they weren't being genuine. Through her travels, Lisa learned how much locals had to share with tourists. Lisa created the Greater Than a Tourist book series to help connect people with locals. A topic that locals are very passionate about sharing.

TABLE OF CONTENTS

ABOUT THE AUTHOR

Isaiah Tribelhorn was born and raised in the greater Kansas City area and has lived in both the suburbs and the heart of downtown. He has traveled to many cities across the nation and a few beyond the US borders but continues to call Kansas City home. When he's not traveling or writing he likes to spend his time cooking, reading, and hosting dinner parties for his friends.

HOW TO USE THIS BOOK

The *Greater Than a Tourist* book series was written by someone who has lived in an area for over three months. The goal of this book is to help travelers either dream or experience different locations by providing opinions from a local. The author has made suggestions based on their own experiences. Please check before traveling to the area in case the suggested places are unavailable.

Travel Advisories: As a first step in planning any trip abroad, check the Travel Advisories for your intended destination.
https://travel.state.gov/content/travel/en/traveladvisories/traveladvisories.html

FROM THE PUBLISHER

Traveling can be one of the most important parts of a person's life. The anticipation and memories that you have are some of the best. As a publisher of the Greater Than a Tourist, as well as the popular *50 Things to Know* book series, we strive to help you learn about new places, spark your imagination, and inspire you. Wherever you are and whatever you do I wish you safe, fun, and inspiring travel.

Lisa Rusczyk Ed. D.
CZYK Publishing

WELCOME TO
> TOURIST

Kansas City Pioneer Square monument in Westport features Pony Express founder Alexander Majors, Westport/Kansas City founder John Calvin McCoy, and Mountain-man Jim Bridger who owned Chouteau's Store.

View of downtown from Penn Valley Park

Country Club Plaza (view from J.C. Nichols Parway at 47th Street), Kansas City, Missouri

Crown Center, plaza & fountains, Kansas City, Missouri

The world is a book and those
who do not travel read only a page.

\-   Saint Augustine

Having spent my entire life in and around Kansas City I've found that it's an incredibly diverse city with rich culture and numerous locations to discover. Just when I've thought I've discovered everything something new or something that had evaded my sight appears just around the corner. History runs deep in Kansas City: history which might have been forgotten elsewhere, but the locals of this fair city have kept that history alive and well, which lends to the feeling of a bigger, older city like New York or Chicago, yet without the hurried feeling that goes with cities that large. The amount of culture mixed with the relaxed atmosphere makes Kansas City both a great place to visit and a wonderful place to live. If that sounds like your sort of city, here are some tips that will help you navigate your stay.

Kansas City
Climate

	High	Low
January	39	21
February	44	25
March	56	35
April	66	46
May	75	56
June	85	66
July	89	71
August	88	69
September	80	60
October	68	48
November	54	36
December	42	25

GreaterThanaTourist.com

Temperatures are in Fahrenheit degrees.
Source: NOAA

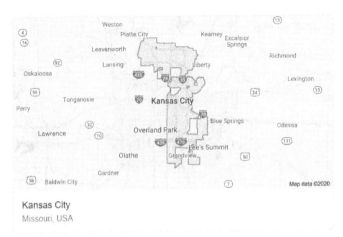

Kansas City
Missouri, USA

WHERE TO STAY AND HOW TO TRAVEL

1. STAYING IN A HOTEL

Downtown Kansas City consists of different districts that all have their own charm. Almost any of them would make a lovely place to stay, however, not all of them have hotels. If hotels are your thing there are a few of them located in the Plaza District, but there are only one or two elsewhere. But not to worry, the Plaza is a lovely place to stay with nearly endless activities and sights to see. The Plaza is one of the prettiest areas in town with amazing architecture and a surprising amount of stone fountains. Simply taking a stroll with a camera can be extremely interesting and satisfying. The Plaza is home to a wide variety of shopping and entertainment. You can find superstores like H&M and small local shops at every turn. Fine seafood restaurants or burger shops can be found with ease, including novelties like Panache Chocolatiers. In the summertime, you'll find buskers performing on the sidewalks and in the squares.

2. STAYING IN AN AIRBNB

If you're up for a stay that's a little more unconventional than a hotel, or if you want to stay in a different area of town that doesn't happen to have a hotel, then an AirBnB is the way to go. There are plenty of affordable and clean spaces to rent for the weekend and this method can put you closer to the center of the city or in a district that sounds particularly interesting. The arts district and the River Market are some lovely areas to stay and explore in your downtime. The River Market is small, cozy, and easy to wander through on foot. The Arts District is a bit larger and easier to get lost in but is full of interesting spaces to discover.

3. A FREE RIDE

Public Transit is popular amongst locals to get around town. One of the big perks of staying in Kansas City is that public transit is totally free. No need for getting weeklong passes or keeping track of tickets, the only trouble you need to go to is learning the bus routes. Once you have those locked down, just find a blue bus and hop on. These bus systems will take you almost anywhere in the downtown area and some of them will even take you to the nearest suburbs.

4. STREETCAR

One of the most popular means of public transit is the streetcar system which is also free. You won't be able to reach every corner of the city on the streetcar, but it covers a good chunk of the city and wait times are minimal between rides. In streetcars, it's polite etiquette to save the seats closest to the doors for the elderly, people in wheelchairs, or pregnant women. Feel free to sit if no one in need is close by, but make sure to keep an eye out for someone who could use a seat close to the door.

Here's a fun game to play: while you're riding the streetcar try and spot the seasoned professionals. You'll recognize them as the people who don't hold onto the rails while it's moving and don't lose their balance when it stops abruptly. You might think this is easy, but it's harder than it looks. If you're feeling daring, try it for yourself, but make sure there's something nearby to grab onto if you stumble.

5. FLYING THROUGH THE STREETS

If you decide to visit in summer you'll find electric scooters to rent on almost every corner. This is my favorite way to get around the city. When you're whizzing across the streets you feel as if you're flying, which is a sensation that's not soon forgotten. Riding one of these in the dog days of summer is also a good way to cool off and rest your legs. These scooters are citywide and can be used late into the night. It's the perfect way to make a late-night ice cream run. These scooters are quick enough that you can cover a large amount of ground in only an hour. Since they don't have any roofs or walls like cars they make for the best views when exploring a new city.

Warning: they do move pretty fast so be careful and be sure to watch for cars and pedestrians.

6. TAKE A WALK

Kansas City is too large to explore solely on foot, but if you're looking to discover neat little areas in a particular district or maybe near where you're staying, I promise you won't be disappointed. Each area of town is filled with things to discover, from specialty ice cream shops to huge three-story antique stores with everything you could dream of. Or maybe you'll discover a cozy coffee shop or a bookstore. No matter where you find yourself you'll be surrounded by beautiful architecture, friendly people, and plenty of interesting spaces to discover. So if you have a few extra hours in your schedule I highly recommend going for a stroll. If you are into taking pictures, make sure to bring your camera with you for some street photography.

7. RIDE KC BIKES

Another good way to get around is the white and orange bicycles you might find racked in certain areas of town. These bikes are available to rent on the spot, or if you're staying for a while you can get a weekly pass. If you don't like taking the bus, this option is more affordable than electric scooters and still gets you around town quickly, although bike stations aren't quite as common as scooters so you may have to walk a little bit to start your biking excursion.

FOOD IS OUR LOVE LANGUAGE

8. COME WITH AN EMPTY STOMACH

Kansas City is home to an amazing amount of delicious restaurants spanning a vast variety of authentic cuisines. Be prepared to gain a few pounds when you come because there will always be one more restaurant to try. Despite living here for my whole life I still haven't even come close to tackling all of the yummy food destinations. On top of that, there's food for every pallet from breakfast diners to cozy French restaurants, Italian delis, and the world-famous Kansas City Barbecue. Once you're finished with the main course be sure to save room for dessert because Kansas City does dessert just as well as it does dinner. One of your biggest challenges when visiting will surely be choosing between all the tasty options.

9. A SACRED THING

When I tell someone I'm from Kansas City the thing they say most often is "how's the barbecue?" Barbecue has been the defining mark placed on the city for decades now, and for good reason. The barbecue in Kansas City is delicious. There are shops all over town, each with their own secret recipes and flavors that define them. Barbecue competitions are prevalent in the summertime and the best restaurants have trophies and awards lining the walls of their shops. But for the locals, barbecue isn't just a thing to be had at restaurants, it's something that people craft at home, striving to perfect their own recipes, even if they never intend to start a restaurant or enter competitions. They spend hours slow-cooking and smoking their meats just for the joy of barbecuing and to share their efforts with friends and family. Barbecue is a point of pride for the people who live here. It's an art form. If you only get to try one restaurant while in town, make it a barbecue joint.

10. JOE'S

It's not unrealistic to say you could stop almost anyone from Kansas City at any time and ask them for a recommendation on barbecue restaurants and each one would happily reply with almost no thought. Each person in Kansas City has had years to come to the conclusion of which place is best. Almost every barbecue place in town is good, but since there are over 100 of them in town it can be hard to choose, and most people have different answers as to which reigns supreme. However only one shop has a legacy that is nearly legend, and that is Joe's. Joe's is undisputedly one of the greats. It started as a tiny shop inside a gas station and eventually grew to its current position as the most well-known barbecue joint in Kansas City. It's not totally uncommon to be in a different state or even a different country and mention Kansas City barbecue only to be greeted with the immediate reply of "Oh yeah, have you been to

TOURIST

Joe's? I hear that place is amazing." Joe's is the essence of Kansas City style barbecue. Once you take your first bite of Joe's you'll know exactly what Kansas City barbecue is all about and I bet you'll fall in love with it. If you get the chance to go you'll most likely find a very long line that often reaches all the way to the door, but don't let that deter you, they're professionals and the line moves quickly. Just stick with it and soon you'll be happy and full. Make sure to get a side of fries with your order. Their special seasoning and perfect cooking method make them my favorite fries in town.

11. BETTY RAE'S

Another eatery that's quickly becoming a legend is Betty Rae's ice cream shop. If you come in the middle of summer the line will be long and slow and it will stay that way until they flip the sign to closed. But there's a reason the line never dies: it's just that good. With an array of flavors ranging from simple vanilla to crazy things like cereal milk and alcoholic white Russian milkshakes, you'll be tempted to visit the shop at least twice before you leave. The ingredients are fresh and delicious and they have a constantly changing menu with new flavors appearing regularly. The shop is only closed for a few weeks in the dead of winter, so even if you're in town when it's chilly, stop by and grab a scoop or two. Just make sure to bundle up to stay cozy while you chow down. Before you leave, write a suggestion for a flavor you'd like to see in the shop and stick it to their pinboard. If you're lucky it will be featured on the menu as one of the next new flavors.

12. A SWEET DRIVE

If you don't mind driving thirty minutes, one of my favorite places on Earth exists in downtown Overland Park, Kansas. The Upper Crust is a pie shop that sells whole pies or pie by-the-slice. The distinct smell hits you as you walk in, sweet fruit mingling with savory pastry crusts and dairy. This quaint little shop will make you feel at home and their pies will make you feel like you never want to leave. Fruit flavors change with the season alongside an array of cream and tart pies, all of which will nearly make you fall out of your chair when you taste the amazing flavors. I dare you to eat only one piece. Ask them to warm a piece of fruit pie up for you and get it a la mode, plus a mug of coffee on the side as a palate cleanser. People say you can't buy happiness, but you can buy the pie at The Upper Crust and I believe that's pretty much the same thing. A few years ago I had the pleasure of sitting at a window seat inside their shop with a mug of coffee and a piece of hot mixed berry pie while rain spattered against the glass. That's a feeling and a memory I won't forget for many years yet. The only thing that could have made that moment more perfect would have been being wrapped in a blanket. This place is a gem.

13. BONBONS

If you like chocolate and trying new things, Christopher Elbow is a local chocolatier who crafts bonbons that look more like modern paintings than food. Each piece is almost unbelievably perfect. But it's not all just show, the flavors are as beautiful as the art. Christopher Elbow is a wizard with flavors, bringing to life things like fresh lemon, rosemary, and strawberry balsamic chocolates. Each bonbon is tempered to perfection, shattering when you bite it revealing the sweet, creamy filling. Truly a treat from a mastermind. You can find these chocolates in their flagship store, as well as any of the Made in KC stores, and select groceries. I recommend visiting the original location which carries more than just bonbons. If you come in winter try out their hot chocolate.

14. BRUNCH

When it comes to food, Kansas City folks love brunch, myself included. This fervent affection for the meal gave birth to many spots devoted solely to brunch, and even more who make sure to serve a stellar brunch menu. One of the top brunch places to check out is Happy Gillis, a family-owned specialty brunch and lunch shop in a small neighborhood called Colombus Park. This shop keeps a small menu and focuses on making every dish perfect. Be sure to try the biscuits and gravy, it might just change your life.

Westport Cafe is a french restaurant and bar that will serve you a tasty exotic brunch menu including Lemon Ricotta Pancakes and Avacado Toast with a poached egg, smoked salmon, and wasabi. Make sure to order one of their cocktails to go with brunch. They are outstanding and a rousing alternative to a traditional mimosa.

15. VEGAN OPTIONS

Most restaurants have one or two vegan options on the menu, but as a whole, Kansas City doesn't have too many restaurants that are specifically vegan. The local favorite option is a bakery called Mud Pie. This quaint cafe and bakery exists inside a repurposed old house alongside one of the busiest streets. The fine folks here provide a variety of savory and sweet offerings as well as coffee and tea. This is one of my personal favorite hangout spots. Grab a vegan cheddar sausage scone, ask them to warm it up for you and head upstairs to one of the quiet little rooms on the second story. The feeling is safe and tucked away from the world. This is one of the best places I know to spend hours chatting or reading.

16. PIZZA AND BEER

Maybe it's late at night and you're looking for something delicious to munch on with a drink, Il Lazzerone has traditional Italian style pizza that they bake in a huge wood fire stove that sits in the middle of the restaurant. You can watch the cooks make and flip the pizza before sliding it into the fiery furnace. For a taste of Italy try the Neapolitan pizza. If you go

39

past the kitchen and head into the back you'll find a beautiful little bar tucked out of sight of the front room. Other than bar seating, this room sports only a few tables and some standing bars for when it gets busy. Despite being in the back of a local pizza shop this bar is considered one of the very best in the city by those in the food industry and is a favorite of the locals. I'm no different, this is my favorite bar in the city as well. The bartenders are wonderful people who know exactly what they're doing and provide an amazing beer and liquor selection as well as top-notch cocktails. If you don't know what to order just ask the bartenders and they will help you pick a cocktail that suits your taste. Most people who walk through the door don't know how to pronounce the somewhat long Italian name and usually butcher it, so here's a useful insider secret that almost no one knows: the owner and everyone who works there never refer to the shop as Il Lazzerone, they only call it Laz. Do the same and people might mistake you for a regular.

17. RESTAURANT WEEK

Every year for a span of ten days, over 200 of Kansas City's finest restaurants participate in an event called Restaurant Week. This fabulous event allows you to order tasting menus that wouldn't normally exist for a much-discounted price. Restaurant Week is a big deal so chefs create two different multiple course menus at two different price points for you to enjoy. For the restaurants, it's a way to get their name out there and show off their spectacular food, and for you, it means delicious and affordable food for ten whole days. If you're planning to come for this make sure to call in reservations at least a week ahead of time. The earlier the better. Tables fill up fast during Restaurant Week. Another way to get a good experience is to reserve a table for an off-peak hour. You can find a list of participating restaurants on Kansas City Restaurant Week's website.

18. FRIENDLY COMPETITION

Alongside the amazing food scene in Kansas City, the people here have endless enthusiasm for their local sports teams. Fairweather fans don't exist in Kansas City, only diehards live in these parts. Even in years where the local teams are at rock bottom fans show tremendous support and excitement for their teams. We show our love by cheering from the bleachers and our love really showed when the football stadium broke the record for the loudest sports stadium ever recorded worldwide and has continued to be the loudest in the nation for multiple years in a row. That's how much we love our teams. When the baseball team won the world series for the first time in thirty years the streets flooded into a sea of blue in celebration. Records show that 800,000 excited fans crammed the streets and sidewalks during the celebration parade. Now that's dedication. Catching a game, whether it be football, baseball, or soccer will give you a local experience unlike any other.

19. THE BEST OF TWO WORLDS

If you happen to visit during football season there's a second side to going to the stadium. It's not all about watching from the bleachers. Tailgating is the art of barbecuing and grilling in the stadium parking lots. It looks like the largest backyard cookout you've ever seen where all the attendants agreed to wear the same color scheme. The symphony of smells, the amazing flavors, and the sea of people all together to have a good time and cheer for their team. It truly is an experience. Over time tailgating has become such an event that many people won't even watch the game, they will go just tailgate. Although most people will roll the windows down in the car and listen to the radio broadcast of the game while they get those perfect grill marks on their steaks. If you have a friend in town, ask them to take you tailgating, it's a tradition that combines two of a Kansas City's favorite things: barbecue and sports.

20. LOCAL MUSIC

There are many music venues in Kansas City, but a popular one amongst the locals is a tiny spot just north of the city called The Rino. The Rino is attached to a small bar, restaurant, and coffee shop that is literally just on the other side of the wall. Usually going to live shows is a bit of an event, but The Rino keeps things casual. Cover charges are usually pretty low, so you won't break the bank to get inside. Conveniently the bar area lends to a relaxed hangout atmosphere. Shows happen here on the regular, so just check the schedule and stop by. It's a great way to discover new artists. If live shows aren't really your thing they also have the occasional stand-up comedy session.

21. RETRO FUN

UpDown is an arcade bar in the center of downtown and is one of the more popular Friday night destinations. Their game selection is second to none, complete with classics like skeeball, Street Fighter, Pac Man, and even an extra-large version of Jenga on the patio. If you are looking to get competitive they have a Nintendo 64 with Mario Kart in the corner. Before you go, try a game called Time Cop. I've spent almost all of my tokens on that one game before playing it for the better part of an hour without stopping. Tokens? That sounds expensive, right? Surprisingly not, tokens are dirt cheap here and you can easily play all night on a budget. If you find yourself with a pile of tokens left at the end of the night and you want to play more, but it's closing time, just stick what you have in your pocket and come back another time. Saving tokens is fair play.

22. RAISING THE STAKES

A relatively new leisure activity that's sweeping the nation is solving escape rooms. Serving as large interactive puzzles the objective is to get out of a locked room with a series of clues that all tie into a central storyline. In most rooms, you aren't actually locked inside, but the door is closed and the decor is often mysterious or spooky. Add in a clock that is counting down to your time limit and you find yourself in an atmosphere that really gets you in the mood for solving mysteries. Kansas City is home to some of the best escape rooms in the country, the shining star of which is Breakout KC in the River

Market district. These rooms are elaborately designed, often with multiple rooms connected by secret doors or tunnels. These rooms are notoriously tricky, so if you want to have your name on the list of those who have beat it, don't underestimate the puzzles they give you. The majority of people who attempt these rooms fail. But even if you don't succeed, solving clues in a crazy, lifesized puzzle box with your friends is a great experience. I highly recommend giving one a try before you head home. You may just get hooked.

23. SILVER DOLLAR CITY

If you have time for a bit of a road trip, Branson, Missouri is only a few hours away and is home to a popular amusement park with strong ties to the great outdoors and times gone by. Branson is a beautiful place to camp and hike, with gorgeous woodlands. Silver Dollar City plays on that and places it's roller coasters in the midst of the trees, which makes for beautiful views from the top. There are winding rivers you can experience on log rides and there is even a cave to explore replete with stalagmites and stalactites. As you walk through the attractions you'll feel as if you've been transported back in time to the days when much of America was undiscovered. This is an all-day or possibly overnight adventure, so make sure you mark off enough time in your schedule to see everything while you're there. Also if you come in summer, make sure to bring some sunscreen and bug spray.

24. AN ADVENTUROUS SPIRIT

If you're the type of person who likes hiking up mountains and through forests, Kansas City holds multiple climbing gyms owned by RoKC. This sport has exploded in popularity over the past few years, and once you go you'll see why; it's loads of fun. I don't think I've met anyone who's tried it and hasn't enjoyed themselves. There's something therapeutic about it. Plus it fulfills all of the times we tried to climb something as children and were told to get down. No one will tell you to get down at these gyms.

The gym selection in Kansas City is hard to go wrong with, all are excellent options and have routes to climb for all experience levels. However, if you want a special experience, there is a smaller location tucked away downtown that is a bit of a secret. If you didn't know where it was, you would never find it ...because it's underground. On the surface, RoKC Underground appears to be just a parking lot with a small one-story structure with the dimensions of an elevator standing in the corner. Surprise! That weird little structure is an elevator, but unlike most elevators, it can only take you under the surface. Once the doors open, you'll find a system of caves much bigger than you would have imagined. Follow the signs that point you down the halls and past many closed doors until you finally arrive at a bouldering-only gym. Bouldering is a type of climbing where you don't climb very high and you don't wear ropes or harnesses. Instead, there are thick, soft mats to fall on. I know falling sounds dangerous, but these gyms are actually quite safe.

The staff at all locations are very friendly and most of them are seasoned climbing veterans who will give you tips and pointers on how to climb in general, or how to complete a particular route you've been working on.

25. CLIMBING LANGUAGE

If you do go climbing you might notice the regulars using a strange climbing jargon. Here are three terms to know when talking to a climber. "Sending" a route means completing a route. All the tenses of "sending" in climbing are the same as they would be when speaking of sending a letter in the mail. You could say "I finally sent that route," or if you're cheering for a friend you might shout "Send it!" The next term is "Beta." The beta of a route is the particular path a climber has chosen to send a route. Routes are much like puzzles with certain steps that are helpful in completing it. Different climbers will have different beta depending on their style, flexibility, and size. The last term is "Crux." Every route has a crux. The crux is the most difficult part of the climb. It might be one tricky hold or reach, or it might be a series of small difficult footholds. If you can get past the crux, you're sure to send a route before the night is over.

26. PICKLEBALL AND FRIED CHICKEN

A sport that a lot of people around town like to play is Pickleball. Not everyone has heard of this sport. It's essentially the halfway step in between table tennis and regulation sized tennis. The rules are almost identical, and the court is similar to a tennis court, only approximately half the size, and instead of rackets and tennis balls, you play with paddles and oversized ping-pong balls. If this sounds like fun to you there is a fried chicken restaurant that has a series of indoor and outdoor courts behind their building that you can rent and play for hours with your friends. You can even bring the food you ordered out to the courts. If you're planning to do this on a weekend you might look into reservations at least a week in advance.

LEISURE TIME

27. A QUIET PLACE

When I travel I love busy cities and all the activities I can manage to squeeze into a day, but sometimes it's also nice to get away from the crowds for a minute and take in a little bit of nature. Loose Park is a beautifully manicured park with a walking trail all the way around it and a rose garden in the center. Take a camera and walk around the peaceful landscape for a few hours and recharge the batteries before heading back into the city. I haven't found many things more peaceful than sitting on one of the benches with my eyes closed, just letting the breeze wash away the stress. If you visit in autumn, this park is transformed into a dazzling show of color that you won't want to miss.

28. EARLY MORNINGS

Mornings can be rough, especially if you're jet-lagged. Sometimes you just don't want to open your eyes and the only thing that can coax you out of bed is the promise of a good cup of coffee. Well, you're in luck. Kansas City has many delightful cafes to visit. If you're looking for a quiet little cafe where you can wake up slow, Splitlog is just the ticket, with a charming rustic aesthetic and a rotating coffee selection, they provide a soothing atmosphere where you can linger and sip your coffee slow. But if you like to jump right into the day without missing a beat, Messenger has a fast-paced environment and a surprisingly large cafe. The building is two stories, plus a rooftop when the weather permits, and each story is immense, making for the largest cafe I've ever experienced. They also have a sister company inside the same building called Ibis that provides baked goods and let me tell you, their pastries are some of the best in Kansas City. There are plenty of places to sit at Messenger, including a few comfy couches where you can sit and watch the hundreds of people pass by, or if it's roasting day you can view the process of how coffee is made and bagged for retail. All the major coffee and baking equipment is out in the open for all to see. And if the patio is open you can look out over a stellar view of the city while you munch a croissant.

29. COFFEE COCKTAILS

Usually, cocktails are made with alcohol, but if you travel fifteen minutes south of the city, you'll find that Second Best Coffee has a line of coffee and tea-based cocktails that change with the season. In summer you might find a jalapeno-mango or grapefruit-pomegranate-mint iced coffee, and in winter their eggnog and white chocolate mixed drink is delicious. They are truly great at what they do, and their baristas will make you feel at home in their clean-cut coffee shop. Before you go grab a cup of cinnamon nitro brew for the road. It's amazing.

30. THE GREAT OUTDOORS

If you like the feel of the sun on your skin and hiking is one of your favorite pastimes, there are some trails up north past the city near Smithville lake. The trails go on for miles and miles and include paved trails plus many offroad varieties for the more adventurous. Depending on how long you want to be out, there are side trails that take a more roundabout path. When totaled all together there are over 14 miles of trails around the lake. Hiking and biking are both welcome. My personal favorite mode of transportation on these trails is a skateboard. Gliding down the gentle hills and around the swooping bends as the trees slowly drift by and the sunlight soaks through the leaves is a magical feeling. It's one of the most peaceful activities I've ever experienced. These trails during autumn are breathtaking and soothing to the soul. Some of the paths run right beside the lake, giving you views of the sparkling water from time to time, making this a delightful excursion. Along these trails, there are also geocaching deposits to be found if you feel like doing a little treasure hunting.

31. WALK ALONG THE RIVER

Berkley Riverfront park offers a short walking trail that runs alongside the river and ends right in front of the River Market District. Watching the river flow endlessly can be a wonderful morning or evening experience. Next to the trail is a park where you might see people doing yoga or playing frisbee. Take a seat on one of the large boulders that decorate the edge of the park and take it all in. Staying fit while on vacation is possible with the outdoor gym equipment located at the far end of the park.

32. BARK

Just beyond the riverside path, there's a building that is both a bar and a dog park. This wonderful location is almost always packed when the weather permits. Its modern chic interior design is both comfortable and clean, while the outside is a cleverly crafted dog park, complete with obstacles and playgrounds for your fluffy friends to play amongst with their new friends. This place is guaranteed to be a good time for dogs and parents alike.

ALCOHOL IS A PASSION

33. A BREWING AND DISTILLING CITY

There numerous alcohol manufacturers and bars in town. Kansas City has been serious about making alcohol since the 1800s, so much so that when the prohibition rolled around Kansas City ignored the new law and continued on as they were for as long as they could. That same passion for the craft continues to this day. If alcohol is your thing, then I'm sure you'll like what Kansas City has to offer. There are

55

tiny breweries that are just getting started where you can pop in and grab a snack and a drink and huge facilities the have guided tours you can take.

34. A PINT OF BEER PLEASE

At the top of the manufacturing chain is Boulevard Brewing who acts as the primary face of local beer. You can tour the brewery or pick up a glass or six-pack at pretty much any bar or grocery store in the city. They serve a full range of types and flavors and they know what they're doing. Check them out if you want a good pint. Their wheat beer is a staple of Kansas City and can be found on almost any menu that serves alcohol.

35. EXPERIMENTS WITH BEER

If you like to live life on the wild side and like your beers to be as crazy as you are, check out Crane brewing. They come out of a small suburb and have become a smash hit across the city. They specialize in beers that pack a punch on your tastebuds, such as a sour that has been infused with berry tea from a local tea company. Their rustic pub aesthetic provides just the right atmosphere to experience a flight of interesting beers in. A paper crane is their logo and will be found on their bottles and glasses.

36. SOMETHING STRONGER

If beer is a little light for your taste Rieger is a distillery that was founded before the prohibition and was eventually shut down sometime after alcohol became illegal and was reopened much later by the founder's descendants using the same recipes. The alcohol here is truly a taste of the past. Cocktails were all the rage in the '20s and Rieger made all their spirits to excel in mixed drinks. To this day Rieger whiskey makes for the best whiskey sour I've ever tasted. Their restaurant and bar can be found inside The Rieger Hotel, which first opened in 1915 and is still an operating hotel with much of the original fixtures and decor still remaining intact.

37. MIX ME A DRINK

The Monarch Bar is a craft cocktail bar with outstanding mixed drinks that are served with beautiful presentations. All this is wrapped up in the stunning interior design and marble bar. The Monarch Bar is sure to impress in every possible way and is one of Kansas City's classiest and most beloved cocktail bars. This is my number one recommendation for a true Kansas City cocktail experience.

38. DRINKS AND A SHOW

Kansas City has a rich culture of brewing and distilling, and some find that goes hand in hand with jazz. Kansas City has been a jazz town for as long as most people can remember and remains so. With a little bit of looking you'll find several jazz bars who have live music till past midnight. One of the most popular destinations is Green Lady Lounge. Contrary to its name, the bar is completely red from top to bottom and has live music all day and late into the night. There's no dress code for this lounge although the dim lighting and prohibition-style decorations combined with classic jazz being played right in front of you will make you feel like you're at a black-tie event. Green Lady has a wide array of drink options but specialize in classic cocktails such as Old Fashioneds and Martinis. This spot can get very busy on weekends but never fear, there is another jazz bar right next door. Black Dolphin is literally a few steps away and is under the same ownership as Green Lady and has a very similar style. Most people prefer Green Lady by a slim margin due to the slight aesthetic differences, so if there's room try Green Lady first.

SEASONAL ACTIVITIES

39. CHINESE NEW YEAR FESTIVAL

There are several large festivals each year in Kansas City, one of which is held at The Nelson Atkins Museum of Art. Whenever Chinese New Year comes around The Nelson Atkins doesn't hold back, they decorate everything all the way to the ceiling. In come many vendors and food stalls, and thus the festival begins. Thousands of people from all across the city come to join the activities and witness the bright colors everywhere and see the performances and taste the delicious foods. Events go on all day, including the famous dragon dances. Like most events at The Nelson, there is no cover charge.

40. BOULEVARDIA

Of all the events Boulevardia is one of the largest. Over 50 musical groups play across three stages. There are yard games, such as cornhole and Connect Four, a Ferris wheel, more beer and food than you could possibly consume, and the recent addition of a silent disco in the evening. It is a quintessential summer festival, and as one of the largest in the city, it's not one to be missed.

41. FIRST FRIDAYS

First Fridays are the most common and traditional festivals in Kansas City. Just like you would assume, they happen on the first Friday of every month. Not everyone or every shop participates in these, but a lot do. As a rule of thumb, there are two halves to the events of the day: the morning and afternoon activities usually happen in the West Bottoms section of town. Pop up food booths and food trucks, art, and merchandise vendors set up shop and certain stores will have special events or sales. Once evening comes on the activities move down to The Crossroads District. First Fridays are most popular during the summer. Some people will even take the day off from work to be able to experience as much of it as they can at these events. First Fridays are a good opportunity to discover local creators and artists, as well as eat a lot of yummy street food.

42. SPOOKY SEASON

If you are in town in October, there are some legitimately spooky haunted houses to walk through. The Beast, and The Edge of Hell are two of the most popular options. These houses are dedicated to the scare and take Halloween seriously, creating elaborate houses with beautifully haunting and delightfully fun rooms that will send the chills down your spine. Haunted houses in Kansas City were among the first to use the design of an open haunted house that allows the participants to explore the house in any way they want, leaving the path they take totally up to them instead of funneling them through rooms in a specific order.

43. CHRISTMAS IN THE PARK

A winter seasonal treat is located just south of the city. Christmas in the Park is a wonderful show of the city's festive spirit. Part of what makes it unique is that you don't have to brave the cold weather and walk the park on foot, it's all designed so that you can stay in your car and keep the heater on. All the dazzling lights and displays are alongside and sometimes over the road. Out of all the Christmas lightings, this is a local favorite. If you decide to attend, patience is key. It's a popular event so the drive will be slow. For the best experience, crank up the Christmas music and don't forget to pick up a cup of hot chocolate before you head in.

44. PLAZA LIGHTING CEREMONY

Kansas City loves Christmas so much that we can't wait for December to arrive so we can get festive. The night of Thanksgiving, as soon as we have napped off the turkey, we head to the Plaza for the lighting ceremony. The Plaza is already a beautiful area of town, but when it's sparkling in seasonal colors it's beyond gorgeous. For this event, there's live music and local celebrities who entertain the crowds until the countdown comes along. At the count of zero, the switch is flipped and the lights come to life. The atmosphere of the event is very similar to a New Years' Eve celebration. When the lights do turn on for the first time, you'll feel as if you've been transported to a town in the North Pole. The tall stone spires glistening in red and green will begin to resemble gingerbread houses, and trees will remind you of gumdrops. Everyone cheers as the Christmas music plays, and we begin to feel as if the Christmas season is finally here. Make sure to grab a cup of cider for this event.

PLACES THAT ARE PART OF US

45. CENTRAL LIBRARY

Among my favorite locations is the downtown library. Made of beautiful stonework it stands five stories tall with a rooftop patio. As you walk through it you might feel as if you are in a museum. Sculptures and pieces of art are hung on the walls and stand atop certain shelves. There are quiet rooms and research rooms made of dark wood that feel as if they

63

belong in a colonial mansion. Occasionally there are special screenings in a private theater room located inside a vault. This vault can be rented for private events. This library is magnificent and is a pleasure to walk through even if you have no intention of picking up a book.

46. THE NELSON ATKINS MUSEUM OF ART

One of the most adored spots of visitors and locals alike is the Nelson Atkins Museum of Art. This museum is one of a national level of quality on par with those in New York. Almost everything about the Nelson Atkins is breathtaking. The building itself is exquisite, the lawn has walking paths that lead to outdoor exhibits and sculptures, some of which are interactive. The landscaping is beautiful. It is sublime to sit on one of the staircases and look out over the lawn. If you go there you might be a little confused at the sight of huge shuttlecocks scattered here and there across the lawns on either side of the museum. These permanent fixtures weren't always intended to be there, they were invented when a couple of artists were hired to put something on the lawn. They decided that the structure and mood of the museum were too rigid and cold and they wanted to lighten the mood. They toyed with ideas, narrowing it down to some sort of game. Basketball was in the running for a while, but they finally settled on badminton shuttlecocks due to the light and whimsical appearance. Since their installment, the shuttlecocks have become iconic symbols representing the museum and Kansas City itself. Some say that if you view the museum from above, the building appears as a white net in the middle of the lawn scattered with shuttlecocks as if a giant game of badminton has just been finished.

The collection of art inside the museum is well curated and moving. The exhibits consist of everything from ancient Egyptian displays to modern art, as well as a rotating exhibit in a separate wing of the building. It's easy to get lost in a world of inspired thought when walking through the Nelson Atkins. Visiting is free of charge, with the only exception being the rotating exhibit which has a small entrance fee. This wondrous world of art and magic is and always will be a pillar of Kansas City. When you arrive, try wearing a pair of headphones as you travel through the exhibits. When you are able to tune out the chatter around you, you will soon find yourself lost in the art.

Be sure to check the events page. Events are happening all the time at The Nelson.

47. SCIENCE CITY

Science City is meant to be a children's museum, but who are we kidding? Adults love it too. This charming museum exists inside of Union Station. You can get to Union Station by streetcar. This was once a busy train station back when trains were the main mode of transport and was built to be a grand showpiece for Kansas City. Nowadays you can still book a train ticket, but the majority of the station is filled with other things such as restaurants, gift shops, and exhibits. One of the exhibits is a rotating display, and the other is Science City. I have loved Science City since I was barely able to walk, and the charm hasn't died even now that I'm grown. Since it was built for children, almost all of the pieces are interactive and allow you to discover the physics of water and air first hand. There's even a piece that allows you to ride a bicycle fifteen feet across the surface of a single rope suspended above the ground, demonstrating how strategically added weight can stabilize your balance. This museum is one of the most interesting and charming I've ever been to.

48. A PLACE FOR HISTORY BUFFS

In addition to the Nelson Atkins Museum of Art and Science City, Kansas City boasts several other historical opportunities. The WWI museum holds the most WWI artifacts out of any museum in the world save Britain's Imperial War Museum. Take a tour through the history of jazz in Kansas City's American Jazz Museum. The Steamboat Arabia museum houses pristine condition artifacts from a steamboat that went down in the Missouri River. The Negro League Baseball Museum shows the history of the Kansas City Monarchs, the team of baseball legend and first African American major league player Jackie Robinson. All are worth checking out.

SHOPPING AND SOUVENIRS

49. SOUVENIRS TO BRING BACK

I'm sure clothing and accessories with a city's initials or the local sports team logo seem cliche, but in Kansas City, it is anything but. Shirts, hats, and sweaters with KC embroidered on them are a daily sight for people who live here. If you ask anyone you see sporting a town logo they'll tell you that they just really like Kansas City and they're proud to represent it. So grab something with the city on it and wear it next time you're in town and I guarantee everyone will think you're a native.

50. LOST IN THE SAUCE

Another good souvenir is bottles of Kansas City barbecue sauce. There are too many spots to try all at once and rather than taking years to try all of them on different trips, why not pick up a little bit of sauce from a lot of different places? Almost all grocery stores carry loads of different local sauces that you can pile into your cart and take home with you. It's also a good way to share an authentic Kansas City experience with your friends. Buy some fried chicken, pour some of all of them into cups and get to dipping, Kansas City style.

BONUS TIP 1: LOCAL CLOTHES AND MERCHANDISE

Locally made clothing, accessories, foods, and drinks can be found in one place. Made in KC stores are dedicated to selling only goods made in Kansas City, from whiskey made by local distilleries, to chocolates, art, and coffee, this store has it all. Their flagship location is complete with a cafe serving local coffee and espresso, and a bar with all the local drinks in the back. If you need some merchandise, souvenirs, or your time is limited and you want to experience as much of Kansas City's consumable offerings as you can, stop by.

BONUS TIP 2: VINTAGE BOUTIQUES

Downtown Kansas City has strong opinions on caring for the ecosystem, recycling, and style. All these things come together in the form of thrifting. Rather than going out to buy new clothes, a lot of people like to shop at one of the various vintage shops. A common favorite is Arizona Trading Company. This boutique has a beautifully curated selection of clothing that will add a pop of vintage style to your wardrobe. When I go shopping, my favorite thing to do is stop by a coffee shop called Oddly Correct that is a few blocks up the road, grab a cup to-go, and walk on down to ATC as the locals call it. Here you will be able to find a nice variety of clothing from the 70s, 80s, and 90s.

BONUS TIP 3: THE SISTER CITIES

Some people like to think of both Kansas City, Missouri and Kansas City, Kansas as one and the same, and some don't even know that there is a Missouri side. However, they are two separate cities and most locals find them to be very different. People who aren't from around here tend to think that Kansas City is located in Kansas. Actually, when most people mention Kansas City, they're speaking of the Missouri side, sometimes without even knowing it.

A little known fact is that despite the shared name, Kansas City, Missouri came before Kansas City, Kansas. The Missouri side was founded as a port city along the river and was called Kansas City after the Kansa Indians. Kansas City began to rapidly grow. When Wyandotte, Kansas saw the success of the city across the way, they decided to also name their city Kansas City in an attempt to join themselves to the successful Missouri city. Some folks from Kansas also felt that they had more rights to the name Kansas City than those on the Missouri side. Even today the two halves of the city are very different. The Kansas side is much smaller and doesn't have a large business district with skyscrapers like its sister city. But what it lacks in skyscrapers it makes up for in delicious food such as the amazing authentic Mexican cuisine the likes of which can't be found on the Missouri side. Plus Kansas City, Kansas is home to my personal favorite barbecue spot called Slaps. While the two cities are very different they both have their charms. When visiting Kansas City you might pop over to the Kansas side for one reason or another, but as the Missouri side is much larger, most of your time will be spent there.

TOP REASONS TO BOOK THIS TRIP

Food: The food is absolutely outstanding, especially the barbecue.

Drinks. There are so many breweries, distilleries, and cocktail bars to try and they're all excellent.

History: The history in the museums is both beautiful and enlightening.

Jazz. Some people think jazz has been condemned to elevator music, but not here in Kansas City. It's all around, and experiencing live jazz is something to remember.

Accessibility. The city is small enough and the public transportation is good enough that you can wander almost every street, exploring each area to the max, discovering hidden gems. This might be the best way to get to know a new city.

DID YOU KNOW?

Kansas City has more fountains than any other city in the world except for Rome

Hallmark began when Joyce Hall started selling postcards out of shoeboxes at a YMCA in Kansas City

At least four US presidents have eaten at the original location of Arthur Bryant's Barbecue

OTHER RESOURCES:

How to get around:
https://ridekc.org/

General info:
https://www.visitkc.com/

Restaurant Week info:
https://www.kcrestaurantweek.com/

TRIVIA

1) Name two celebrities who came from Kansas City

2) Which came first, Kansas City, Missouri? Or Kansas City, Kansas?

3) How many people live in Kansas City?

4) What national law did Kansas City ignore in the 1920s?

5) Which famous animator opened their first animation studio in Kansas City?

6) What is the record for inches of snowfall in a single day in Kansas City?

7) What frozen dessert was invented in Kansas City?

8) Kansas City holds over how many barbecue restaurants?

9) Which famous author was a cub reporter for the Kansas City Star newspaper from 1917 to 1918?

10) Which Kansas City park is more than twice the size of Central Park in New York?

ANSWERS

1) Paul Rudd, Don Cheadle, Rob Riggle, Ellie Kemper

2) Kansas City, Missouri was born in 1853. Kansas City, Kansas was founded in 1872

3) Almost 500,000

4) In the 1920s Kansas City ignored the prohibition and continued to serve alcohol

5) Walt Disney opened his first animation studio in Kansas City

6) On March 23rd, 1912, Kansas City accumulated 20.5 inches of snowfall in a single day

7) Bomb Pops

8) Over 100 barbecue restaurants

9) Ernest Hemingway

10) Swope Park

PACKING AND PLANNING TIPS

A Week before Leaving

- Arrange for someone to take care of pets and water plants.

- Email and Print important Documents.

- Get Visa and vaccines if needed.

- Check for travel warnings.

- Stop mail and newspaper.

- Notify Credit Card companies where you are going.

- Passports and photo identification is up to date.

- Pay bills.

- Copy important items and download travel Apps.

- Start collecting small bills for tips.

- Have post office hold mail while you are away.

- Check weather for the week.

- Car inspected, oil is changed, and tires have the correct pressure.

- Check airline luggage restrictions.

- Download Apps needed for your trip.

Right Before Leaving

- Contact bank and credit cards to tell them your location.

- Clean out refrigerator.

- Empty garbage cans.

- Lock windows.

- Make sure you have the proper identification with you.

- Bring cash for tips.

- Remember travel documents.

- Lock door behind you.

- Remember wallet.

- Unplug items in house and pack chargers.

- Change your thermostat settings.

- Charge electronics, and prepare camera memory cards.

READ OTHER GREATER THAN A TOURIST BOOKS

Greater Than a Tourist- Geneva Switzerland: 50 Travel Tips from a Local by Amalia Kartika

Greater Than a Tourist- St. Croix US Birgin Islands USA: 50 Travel Tips from a Local by Tracy Birdsall

Greater Than a Tourist- San Juan Puerto Rico: 50 Travel Tips from a Local by Melissa Tait

Greater Than a Tourist – Lake George Area New York USA: 50 Travel Tips from a Local by Janine Hirschklau

Greater Than a Tourist – Monterey California United States: 50 Travel Tips from a Local by Katie Begley

Greater Than a Tourist – Chanai Crete Greece: 50 Travel Tips from a Local by Dimitra Papagrigoraki

Greater Than a Tourist – The Garden Route Western Cape Province South Africa: 50 Travel Tips from a Local by Li-Anne McGregor van Aardt

Greater Than a Tourist – Sevilla Andalusia Spain: 50 Travel Tips from a Local by Gabi Gazon

Children's Book: *Charlie the Cavalier Travels the World* by Lisa Rusczyk Ed. D.

> TOURIST

Follow us on Instagram for beautiful travel images:
http://Instagram.com/GreaterThanATourist

Follow *Greater Than a Tourist* on Amazon.

>Tourist Podcast

>T Website

>T Youtube

>T Facebook

>T Goodreads

>T Amazon

>T Mailing List

>T Pinterest

>T Instagram

>T Twitter

>T SoundCloud

>T LinkedIn

>T Map

> TOURIST

At *Greater Than a Tourist*, we love to share travel tips with you. How did we do? What guidance do you have for how we can give you better advice for your next trip? Please send your feedback to GreaterThanaTourist@gmail.com as we continue to improve the series. We appreciate your constructive feedback. Thank you.

METRIC CONVERSIONS

TEMPERATURE

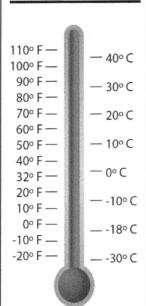

110° F — — 40° C
100° F —
90° F — — 30° C
80° F —
70° F — — 20° C
60° F —
50° F — — 10° C
40° F —
32° F — — 0° C
20° F —
10° F — — -10° C
0° F —
-10° F — — -18° C
-20° F — — -30° C

To convert F to C:

Subtract 32, and then multiply by 5/9 or .5555.

To Convert C to F:

Multiply by 1.8 and then add 32.

32F = 0C

LIQUID VOLUME

To Convert:...................Multiply by
U.S. Gallons to Liters................. 3.8
U.S. Liters to Gallons 26
Imperial Gallons to U.S. Gallons 1.2
Imperial Gallons to Liters....... 4.55
Liters to Imperial Gallons 22
1 Liter = .26 U.S. Gallon
1 U.S. Gallon = 3.8 Liters

DISTANCE

To convert ....Multiply by
Inches to Centimeters 2.54
Centimeters to Inches 39
Feet to Meters........................ .3
Meters to Feet 3.28
Yards to Meters 91
Meters to Yards 1.09
Miles to Kilometers 1.61
Kilometers to Miles............ .62
1 Mile = 1.6 km
1 km = .62 Miles

WEIGHT

1 Ounce = .28 Grams
1 Pound = .4555 Kilograms
1 Gram = .04 Ounce
1 Kilogram = 2.2 Pounds

TRAVEL QUESTIONS

- Do you bring presents home to family or friends after a vacation?

- Do you get motion sick?

- Do you have a favorite billboard?

- Do you know what to do if there is a flat tire?

- Do you like a sun roof open?

- Do you like to eat in the car?

- Do you like to wear sun glasses in the car?

- Do you like toppings on your ice cream?

- Do you use public bathrooms?

- Did you bring a cell phone and does it have power?

- Do you have a form of identification with you?

- Have you ever been pulled over by a cop?

- Have you ever given money to a stranger on a road trip?

- Have you ever taken a road trip with animals?

- Have you ever gone on a vacation alone?

- Have you ever run out of gas?

- If you could move to any place in the world, where would it be?

- If you could travel anywhere in the world, where would you travel?

- If you could travel in any vehicle, which one would it be?

- If you had three things to wish for from a magic genie, what would they be?

- If you have a driver's license, how many times did it take you to pass the test?

- What are you the most afraid of on vacation?

- What do you want to get away from the most when you are on vacation?

- What foods smell bad to you?

- What item do you bring on ever trip with you away from home?

- What makes you sleepy?

- What song would you love to hear on the radio when you're cruising on the highway?

- What travel job would you want the least?

- What will you miss most while you are away from home?

- What is something you always wanted to try?

- What is the best road side attraction that you ever saw?

- What is the farthest distance you ever biked?

- What is the farthest distance you ever walked?

- What is the weirdest thing you needed to buy while on vacation?

- What is your favorite candy?

- What is your favorite color car?

- What is your favorite family vacation?

- What is your favorite food?

- What is your favorite gas station drink or food?

- What is your favorite license plate design?

- What is your favorite restaurant?

- What is your favorite smell?

- What is your favorite song?

- What is your favorite sound that nature makes?

- What is your favorite thing to bring home from a vacation?

- What is your favorite vacation with friends?

- What is your favorite way to relax?

- Where is the farthest place you ever traveled in a car?

- Where is the farthest place you ever went North, South, East and West?

- Where is your favorite place in the world?

- Who is your favorite singer?

- Who taught you how to drive?

- Who will you miss the most while you are away?

- Who if the first person you will contact when you get to your destination?

- Who brought you on your first vacation?

- Who likes to travel the most in your life?

- Would you rather be hot or cold?

- Would you rather drive above, below, or at the speed limited?

- Would you rather drive on a highway or a back road?

- Would you rather go on a train or a boat?

- Would you rather go to the beach or the woods?

TRAVEL BUCKET LIST

1.

2.

3.

4.

5.

6.

7.

8.

9.

10.

NOTES

CPSIA information can be obtained
at www.ICGtesting.com
Printed in the USA
LVHW040228190620
658491LV00007B/1665